Donated by

The Flock Family

P is for Potato

An Idaho Alphabet

Written by Stan and Joy Steiner and Illustrated by Jocelyn Slack

Sleeping Bear Press

310 North Main Street, Suite 300
Chelsea, MI 48118
www.sleepingbearpress.com

THOMSON

GALE

© 2005 Thomson Gale, a part of the Thomson Corporation.

Thomson, Star Logo and Sleeping Bear Press are trademarks
and Gale is a registered trademark used herein under license.

Printed and bound in Canada.

10 9 8 7 6 5 4 3 2 1

Library of Congress Cataloging-in-Publication Data

Steiner, Joy.
P is for potato : an Idaho alphabet / written by Joy and Stan Steiner ; illustrated
by Jocelyn Slack.
p. cm.
Summary: "An A-Z pictorial for children ages 4-10 all about Idaho including,
famous people, geography, history, and state symbols. Letter topics are introduced
with poems accompanied by expository text to provide detailed information"—
Provided by publisher.
ISBN 1-58536-155-0
1. English language—Alphabet—Juvenile literature. 2. Idaho—Juvenile literature.
I. Steiner, Stanley F. II. Slack, Jocelyn. III. Title.
F746.3.S745 2005
979.6—dc22   2004028838

*We dedicate this book to the Idaho teachers, librarians, parents,
and students who inspire others to read. We offer a special thank-you
to Marie and Roland Smith, and Ben, Lea, and Avi Steiner.*

STAN and JOY

for John and Luna

JOCELYN

A is for Appaloosa steed,
Idaho's own magnificent breed,
developed by the Nez Perce tribe,
a horse of intelligence, beauty, and speed.

Sik'em is the Nez Perce word for horse. Although the Nez Perce were not the first tribe to have horses, they were the first to develop a breed with the qualities they needed. With such a fine horse, Nez Perce hunters traveled the long Lolo Trail to Montana for a yearly bison hunt. At full gallop, warriors shot their arrows with amazing accuracy while hanging beneath the neck of their sturdy *sik'em*. European American settlers called the horse a Palousey pony when they saw them grazing on the rich grasses of the Palouse country. The Appaloosa is now Idaho's state horse with a coat that ranges from white-blanketed hips to full leopard spots.

The Idaho state fossil is also a horse, but it is much older than the Appaloosa. The Hagerman Horse, 3,500,000 years old, is smaller than modern horses and closely related to a zebra. The bones can be seen at Hagerman Fossil Beds National Monument, one of the best Pleistocene era fossil sites in the world.

B is for Boise, city of trees,
the capital of Idaho.
A river runs through the middle of town,
where herons go fishing with hardly a sound.

Boise has been known as the city of trees since the days of the French trappers. The city was built around the Boise River, where tall, shady cottonwood trees were a welcome sight for trappers and pioneers crossing Idaho's desert. City fathers began a tradition of planting trees which continues as an urban forestry program. Boise is a beautiful state capital with bustling city life, yet plenty of open space for hiking and biking. There is a zoo, art exhibits and performances, ice hockey and baseball teams, and a thriving university. In spite of all the city activity, the Boise River flows calmly past, providing a home for bald eagles, great blue herons, and a place to quietly fish or float in an old inner tube.

Our capitol building is the only one in the United States heated by geothermal energy. Naturally hot water is piped from deep underground to the capitol, completed in 1920. Geothermal energy is an inexpensive way to heat a large space.

C is for Craters of the Moon—
a national monument.
It was formed by lava long ago,
a land of black rock, twisted and bent.

Craters of the Moon is really quite young in geological years. A large crack opened in the Earth some 2,000 years ago, forming several volcanoes which erupted and spit and flowed into many different rock shapes. Ancient people came to the lava flows to find shiny black tachylite rock for making arrow points. Today's visitors can hike and explore the formations and lava tunnels. Pahoehoe lava is smooth and ropey, but watch out for Aa; it's jagged and sharp on the feet!

Craters of the Moon is close to Arco, the world's first atomic town. In 1951 the nearby National Reactor Testing Station was the first in the world to produce electricity from nuclear fission. Four years later, the lights of Arco were lit by nuclear energy alone. The testing station is now called Idaho National Engineering and Environmental Laboratory, still on the cutting edge of energy research.

It took thousands of years to form Hells Canyon. The Snake River cut into old volcanic rock between the Wallowa Mountains in Oregon and the Seven Devils in Idaho. In some places Hells Canyon is 7,900 feet, the deepest river gorge in North America. A national recreation area, visitors can boat and fish on the Snake River, explore ancient petro-glyphs on the rocks, and watch for wildlife. Once Nez Perce country, this is the flood-swollen river Chief Joseph was forced to cross with his people when the U.S. Cavalry pushed them onto reservation land in 1877. Amazingly, not a person was drowned in the crossing, not even the women and children, who floated swiftly to the far shore in their animal skin boats.

D is also for dunes made of sand. Bruneau Sand Dunes State Park, near Mountain Home, is a great place to camp and play. Visitors tumble and sled on the dune by day and watch stars from the remarkable observatory by night.

D d

D is the Deepest river gorge.
Hells Canyon was formed many years ago.
The mighty Snake River flooded and flowed,
and wore down the rock far below.

E e

The Idaho state seal is the only one in the United States designed by a woman. Emma Edwards, a newcomer to Boise and just out of art school, entered a state-sponsored contest for the Idaho seal. Her design was unanimously chosen as the favorite. Miss Edwards was awarded $100 in prize money and her design was adopted by the Idaho state legislature in 1891.

The Idaho state seal is lettered with the motto "*Esto Perpetua*," the hope that the beautiful lands of Idaho will "last forever." Our state flag also carries the state seal set on a blue background.

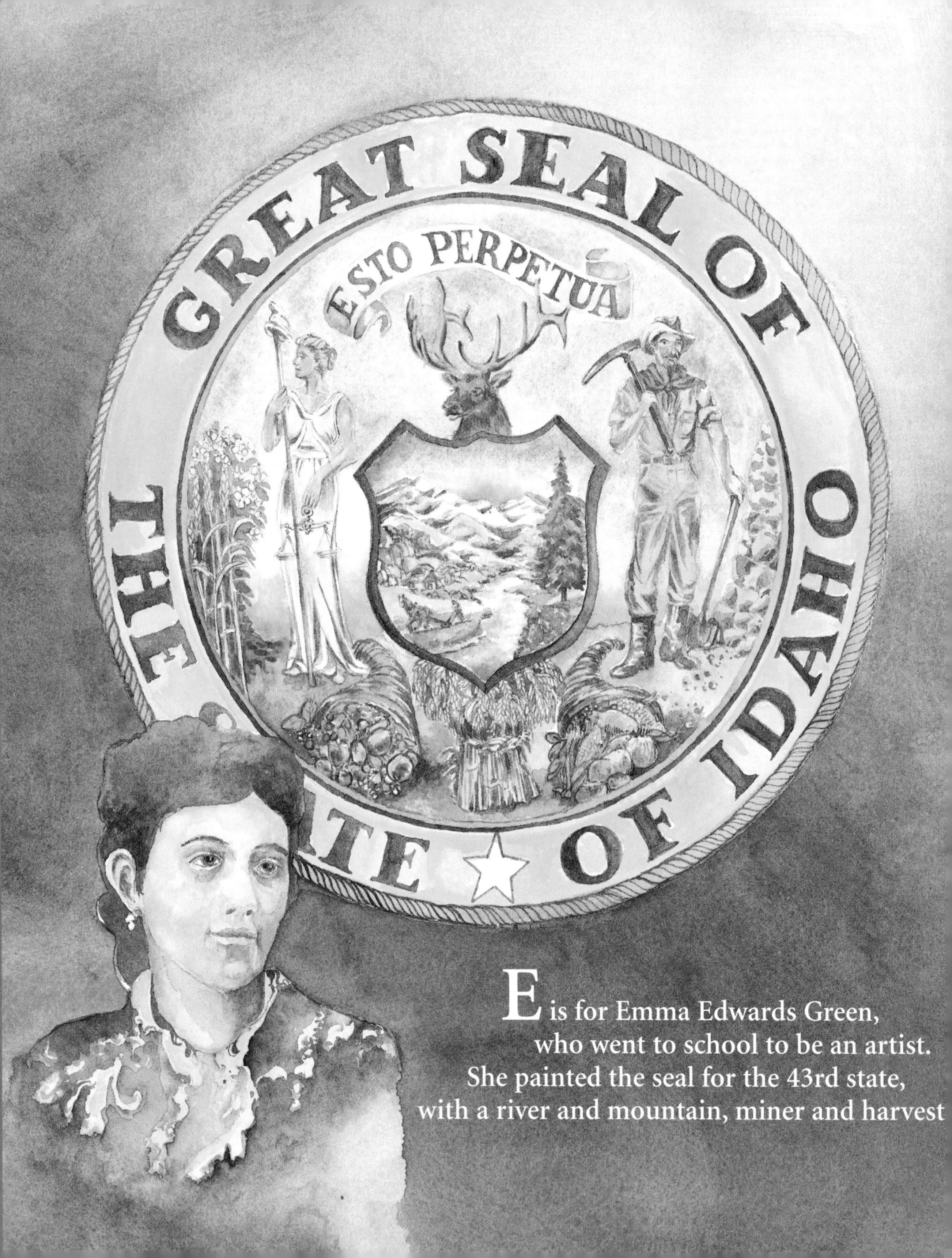

GREAT SEAL OF
ESTO PERPETUA
THE ☆ TE OF IDAHO

E is for Emma Edwards Green,
who went to school to be an artist.
She painted the seal for the 43rd state,
with a river and mountain, miner and harvest.

Idaho has the largest stand of western white pine in the nation. It is no wonder that it was chosen as the state tree! Idaho has 21 million acres of national forest. Also growing in the forests are ponderosa pine, spruce, Douglas fir, and white fir. These forests provide a home to many animals, but the lands are also used for mining, logging, recreation, and watershed protection.

Devoto Memorial Cedar Grove and Hobo Cedar Grove Botanical Area are protected forests growing in moist areas of northern Idaho. The majestic trees in these forests are 1,000 years old, but there are others in Idaho which are older. Growing in pockets of deep ash soil which drifted into Idaho from ancient volcanic eruptions are trees which sprouted 3,000 years ago. Fragrant and peaceful, these old cedar trees urge us to breathe deeply, leave our cares behind, and take good care of our beautiful earth.

Bristly branches, towering trees,
animal homes, flowing streams—
follow the path, smell the air,
F is a Forest, lovely and rare.

If you dig the dirt in just the right spot,
you might find a treasure that's worth a lot.
We have garnets and opals and flakes of gold.
G is for Gem State, that's Idaho.

LAKE
COEUR
D'ALENE

EMERALD CREEK
GARNET AREA

Idaho truly earns its nickname, the Gem State. Opals, agates, garnets, and more can be found in soil created long ago by volcanoes and water. Star garnets are more valuable than rubies or sapphires. These deep red and purple crystals reflect a fascinating six-point star. Because they are found in only two places in the world, Idaho and India, star garnets are the Idaho state gem.

G is also for gold, the mineral that changed Idaho forever. Few settlers were interested in coming to this rugged region, but when gold was found in 1860 near Pierce, the population exploded. Miners from America, Europe, and China flocked from claim to claim, setting up camps which became Florence, Idaho City, and Silver City. Conflicts arose between the miners and those who lived there first, leading to the tragic Nez Perce Wars. Railroads came to service the mines and logging operations. Towns sprang up, and Idaho became a state just 30 years after gold was discovered.

Imagine a swimming pool as warm as a bath tub. Imagine skiing or walking through the snow, taking off your warm winter clothes, and jumping into steamy warm water! It is a fun, free gift from nature!

Idaho has the right geology for natural hot springs. There is plenty of underground water, and deep cracks where the water can flow closer to the Earth's hot core before coming back to the surface. There are hot springs all over the state from Lava and Lolo to Gibbons and Zims and Burgdorf. Swim safely, though. Make sure there is cool water flowing nearby to keep the temperature comfortable and choose your swimming partners carefully. Someone brought alligators all the way to Thousand Springs to enjoy the hot water, too!

H h

H
Splash on in and soak awhile,
is a Hot tub, natural style.
Hot water springs from deep underground
make a pool you can swim in all year round.

Idaho is famous for growing tons of potatoes, but farmers couldn't grow them without plenty of water. Potatoes are thirsty plants. Since most of Idaho is a dry desert, farmers borrow water from rivers and underground lakes called aquifers. These water resources help farmers grow not only potatoes, but also peas, wheat, fruit, and sugar beets. There is another important crop as well. Idaho is the nation's number one producer of farmed trout.

Irrigation is a way of life in Idaho. Water resources in Idaho have been actively harnessed since 1836, when Presbyterian missionary Henry Spalding convinced Nez Perce people to dig irrigation ditches and grow potatoes to add to their already nutritious diet of salmon and camas root. Mormon settlers developed irrigation along the Lemhi river in 1855, but the most impressive water project in the early days was the New York Canal, named after its New York financers. Finished in 1900, it supplied water for farming all over the Boise area. A flurry of dam-building projects from 1930 to 1968 altered waterways and increased the population and prosperity of southern Idaho, home to the state's largest cities.

Ii

I is for Irrigating crops
which helps the plants to grow.
Farmers get water from rivers and lakes.
The land is too dry in Idaho.

J is for June when syringa blooms
with a fragrance so sweet it could fill a room.
Snowy white blossoms on each bough,
syringa is Idaho's lovely state flower.

The syringa is just like Idaho, rugged and beautiful. It doesn't mind the dry arid weather of the west and is happy to grow tall near the forest where animals can hide among its leafy branches. Creamy white syringa blossoms are fragrant and attractive. Early people used the leaves to make soap and the branches for arrow shafts. Chosen by the Idaho legislature, syringa is a lovely choice for the state flower.

Jj

Ketchum is our word for **K**,
a wonderful place to ski and play.
Powdery snow brings skiers west,
Sun Valley is how we know it best.

Ketchum was once a lead and silver mining town. When the mines stopped producing, people moved on to find better jobs. Ketchum became a quiet little sheep ranching town with a train that stopped twice a week. But the chairman of the Union Pacific Railroad got an idea. Averell Harriman had heard about a popular European sport called skiing, and convinced the railroad to create a resort accessible by train. Within a year the land was bought and the lodge was built. The world's first chairlift was installed, and in 1936 Sun Valley ski resort was born.

Picabo Street won the 1998 Olympic gold medal for ski racing in Nagano, Japan. Picabo graduated from high school in Ketchum and trained on the slopes of Sun Valley. As a girl, Picabo developed her competitive spirit by outracing all the boys. That spirit served her well through devastating injuries and triumphant comebacks. Her story is a fine example of the American dream: a small-town girl wins big!

Fishing is a popular sport in Idaho. Rainbow trout, bull trout, and cutthroat trout, the state fish, swim the cold waters of Idaho's rivers. Once abundant, some salmon still make the amazing journey from their years in the ocean, returning to their wild Idaho birthplace to spawn and die.

L is also for leader. Moses Alexander was the United States' first Jewish governor. Alexander immigrated from Germany when he was 14 and became an American citizen. A gifted manager, he opened his first clothing shop in Boise, and was so successful his business expanded to include a chain of 10 clothing stores along the railway route from Twin Falls to Vale, Oregon. Alexander was voted governor in 1914, during WWI. He urged Idaho farmers to grow extra crops to feed the soldiers and prevented strikes by union workers in the mines and forests. Soon Idaho minerals, lumber, and food were helping the United States and her allies to win WWI.

L l

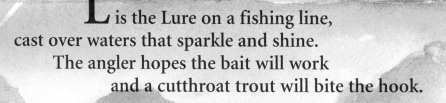

L is the Lure on a fishing line,
cast over waters that sparkle and shine.
The angler hopes the bait will work
and a cutthroat trout will bite the hook.

Mount Borah and Monarch butterfly,
our choices for **M** decorate the sky,
and a bright shock of blue flies swiftly past.
It's the Mountain bluebird, returning at last.

M
m

Mount Borah is the highest peak in Idaho, at 12,622 feet. It is named for William Borah, congressman from 1907 to 1940, and Idaho's first presidential candidate. Mount Borah gained a foot in 1983, when an earthquake measuring 7.3 on the Richter scale cracked and compressed the earth at the base of the peak.

The mountain bluebird and the monarch butterfly are Idaho's state bird and insect. Sturdy travelers, both migrate each year. Mountain bluebirds are all blue with touches of gray underneath. They spend winter in the South, and are a welcome sight each spring, when they return to their mountain homes in a hollow tree or fence post. Monarch butterflies flash their bright orange and black wings as a warning to predators. They are poisonous to eat. Even the caterpillars, whose bodies contain poisons from eating milkweed and dogbane, wear bright stripes to keep animals away. Monarchs live in California and Mexico during winter, but fly north to lay their eggs on milkweed plants.

Native Americans flourished in Idaho for thousands of years before European Americans came. Six main groups populated Idaho including the Kootenai, Kalispel, Coeur d'Alene, Nez Perce, Shoshone, and Bannock. Sometimes these names were given to the tribes by the European American travelers who met them, but most of the tribes named themselves after the food they ate or the place they lived. There were the River People, the Camas People, and the Salmon Eaters. The largest tribe in Idaho, the Nez Perce, simply called themselves *Nimiipuu*, "we the people."

Native Americans made great contributions to Idaho's historic past and continue to shape its future. Chief Tendoy, Chief Joseph, and Chief Egan from the past are fine examples of leaders who gave themselves unselfishly to protect the people. Larry EchoHawk, elected in 1991, influenced policy as our nation's first Native American attorney general.

N n

N is for Native people, the first Americans.
They built their camps and villages all across this land.
They fished its tumbling waters; they gathered plants for food;
they roamed the hills of Idaho, a land they understood.

Many dangers awaited pioneers traveling through Idaho on the Oregon Trail. The cold, fast waters of the Snake River created an enormous challenge. Settlers had to choose the longer arduous route south of the Snake, or prepare their animals and wagons to ford the river, where the land to the north grew better grasses for grazing. Three Island Crossing on the Snake River was most often used. Travelers were deeply weary at this stage in their journey and food supplies were dwindling. Two forts provided shelter and relief. Fort Hall, near present day Pocatello, was a major hub for trails to the west. It was built about 10 years before the immigrants came. Near Parma, where the Boise River empties into the Snake, Fort Boise was a welcome sight for the pioneers. It meant they would soon be in Oregon. Their journey was nearly over.

O is for the Oregon Trail,
　　so hot and dry in Idaho.
　　　　Dust and sage, mile after mile,
　　and still a long, long walk to go.

French fries and hash browns, bakers and chips,
Potato is our word for **P**.
With water, the Idaho desert can grow
spuds for you; spuds for me.

Blackfoot, Idaho grows more potatoes than anywhere else in the world. All along the Snake River Valley farmers use irrigation and fertilizer to raise their famous russet potatoes. Idaho spuds are excellent for making french fries and baking. The state's high altitude and cool nights also produce hardy seed potatoes which resist disease. As long as there is water, Idaho's state vegetable will grow strong.

J. R., "Jack" Simplot is known for his luck with potatoes. Using money earned from selling hogs, young Simplot grew certified quality seed potatoes. He sold his seed, then used the income to invest in land. Simplot's big success came during WWII, when he created a food dehydrating company which supplied the U.S. military with 38 million pounds of dried potatoes and onions to feed the soldiers. Now one of the richest men in America, J. R. Simplot is, above all, a hardworking businessman who has a gift for knowing when and where to invest his money.

P p

Quinceanera is our word for **Q**—
celebrate is what we do.
A girl grows up with love and pride,
her family has been her guide.

Quinceanera is a tradition celebrated by many Latin American families in Idaho. This ceremony began hundreds of years ago with Aztec culture in Mexico. When a girl turned 15 she was asked to choose a life devoted to religion or motherhood. Girls observing their quinceanera today have more choices, but they are still asked to recommit their lives to God and ponder their future. All over North America the tradition of quinceanera continues, as Latin American families celebrate the lives of their daughters. Let the *fiesta* begin!

Hispanic people first came to Idaho in the early 1800s as trappers and adventurers. Those who came a hundred years ago worked the railroads and farms, laboring under the Idaho sun. Today men and women with a Latin American heritage are community leaders in every profession. Nampa is the site of the state's first Hispanic Cultural Center. There, visitors can learn about Hispanic history in Idaho, prominent citizens, traditions, religion, and the cultural arts.

Idaho's rivers are impressive. Six rivers have been given the designation of Wild and Scenic by the United States Congress. Kayaking and rafting adventures abound among the whitewater rapids of the Payette, the Salmon and its tributaries. Senator Frank Church created the River of No Return Wilderness to protect the waters and lands of the Salmon, the longest undammed river within the borders of one state in the lower 48 states. Lewis and Clark decided not to cross the treacherous Salmon when they saw the rapids from an overlooking bluff. The Big Lost River flows into porous lava fields near Arco and disappears into the Snake River aquifer deep underground. The water bursts forth again at the cliffs of Thousand Springs to join the Snake River on its journey to the Columbia River and the Pacific Ocean. Idaho's rivers are invaluable, and have unique qualities worth preserving.

R r

Splash, swim, raft in the sun.
Paddle the rapids for thrilling fun,
or watch a blue heron stalking a fish.
R is a River rushing along.

When Lewis and Clark explored the West,
    one brave young woman assisted their quest.
S   A valuable member of the crew—
    is for Sacajawea.

S s

A young *Agaidika* Shoshone girl from the Lemhi Valley of Idaho was gathering food with her family. Her name was Sacajawea. Suddenly, *Gros Ventre* raiders attacked. They captured Sacajawea and took her far away to the Missouri River. She was sold to an Hidatsa tribe, then sold again as wife to a French-Canadian trapper.

In the autumn of 1804, Lewis and Clark and their Corps of Discovery pushed up the Missouri River. The men built a fort near the Hidatsa people for shelter from the harsh winter. Sacajawea's husband heard that Lewis and Clark would pay money for an interpreter, so he joined the expedition, bringing his pregnant wife along. Sacajawea gave birth to their son during the long winter. When spring came, she was eager to travel. Even with a baby strapped to her back, Sacajawea was a valuable expedition member, providing food, making clothing, and easing the trade with her Lemhi Shoshone people and the Nez Perce for horses the expedition needed. Sacajawea was not really a guide, but her very presence with the baby proved that the Corps of Discovery came in peace.

Science and technology are now the biggest industries for the state of Idaho. Computer hardware manufacturing, software programming, fiber optics, and semiconductor products are just a few state-of-the-art businesses that thrive here. More Idahoans work in "high-tech" industry than in any other profession.

Philo T. Farnsworth of Rigby, Idaho, is known as the Father of Television. In 1920, when he was only 14, an idea came to him while his hands were busy plowing a field. As soon as he could, he chalked his idea on the blackboard and explained it to his high school teacher. It was fortunate that he shared his idea, because his former teacher became a key witness, producing a 1922 sketch that proved Philo Farnsworth deserved the patent as the first to invent television.

T is for Technology,
          computers, and Internet, and the TV.
Many people in Idaho
                    work for a high-tech company.

T t

U u

Union Pacific stands for U.
The railroad came to Idaho.
It opened the West to a brand new plan;
settlers came to claim the land.

The Union Pacific and Central Pacific Railways were joined with a golden spike at Promontory Point, Utah, near Salt Lake City. Eventually Idaho gained its first rail service, the Utah Northern, in 1881. Soon the Oregon Short Line had an east-west hub in Pocatello, and the Northern Pacific crossed the forests of the panhandle. Farm produce, wool, lumber, and minerals were sent out of Idaho and settlers were sent in to homestead the land along the railways.

The railways brought prosperity for some, but sacrifice and loss for others. The great plains buffalo herds had been hunted to near extinction and the native people who had lived with the land for more than 9,000 years were pushed aside to live on reservations. Gone were the wide open spaces the cowboy had enjoyed. Changes came faster and faster, cities grew, factories prospered, and the railroad became the lifeline for American industry.

If someone wants to find a huckleberry patch, the best thing to do is walk in a shady pine forest and breathe deeply. When huckleberries are ripe, they fill the air with clouds of sweet scent. It's wise to keep a sharp lookout for dark furry shapes, though. Hungry bears love huckleberries too, and the forest is their home.

Huckleberries are the Idaho state fruit. They grow best in the wild high places, and love to have a good winter snow cover. It takes a long time for a bush to bear fruit, sometimes 15 years, but it is worth the wait. Even one purple berry, no bigger than a fingertip, bursts with sweet tart flavor. Several hours of picking fills a bucket, but all the work pays off. Huckleberries make wonderful pies, pancakes, muffins, and jam. The Idaho state fruit has a taste that people remember.

V is for *Vaccinium*, yum—
the huckleberry fruit.
If you walk along a wooded trail
be sure to take your pail.

W is a wonderful place,
the World Center for Birds of Prey.
Scientists work to find a way
to help endangered birds survive.

Raptors from every corner of the Earth are carefully raised and rehabilitated at the World Center for Birds of Prey, south of Boise. Raptors are meat-eating birds. They include hawks, falcons, eagles, vultures, and owls. The scientists at the center pioneer ways to raise these fascinating wild birds and release them back to their habitats. The World Center for Birds of Prey is most noted for its ongoing programs to save the peregrine falcon and California condor.

There are many projects in Idaho to help birds survive. Whooping cranes have mingled with sandhill cranes at Gray's Lake Wildlife refuge near Wayan, Idaho, where biologists worked to rescue the stately birds from extinction. Morley Nelson helped establish the Snake River Birds of Prey Conservation Area, a rocky haven for nesting raptors. The Idaho Bird Observatory is dedicated to studying the health of songbirds and the raptors which follow them on their migrations. These hardworking scientists know it is important to keep birds thriving.

A spry, lilting sound tickles your ears,
and makes you want to leap up and dance. X
 It's the txistu, our X word, a three-hole recorder,
brought by Basque people of Spain and France.

The wooden txistu (che-stu) is tradition-ally played in the right hand while the left beats out a lively rhythm on a tambora drum. Such a well-coordinated musician is called a txistulari (che-stu-lah-re). An accordion and tambourine together make a trikitixia (tre-ke-te-sha) band, just right for dancing. This music comes from the Basque culture, which is more than 10,000 years old.

Basque people came to Idaho from the Pyrenees mountains of northern Spain and southern France. Over a hundred years ago, when times were hard in Basque country, young people migrated to America. So many came to Idaho they called it the fifth province of Spain. The Basque people were valued for their hard work and honesty, finding jobs as shepherds, irrigation diggers, and hotel owners. Today the Basque flourish in modern society and proudly take part in their cultural legacy.

X
x

Emma Yearian earns our Y.
She knew how to care for orphaned lambs.
She raised them all with a patient hand
and her sheep ranch grew across the land.

Emma Yearian started with cattle but she became interested in sheep ranching when her husband brought home orphaned lambs for her to care for. She needed more land for the sheep, so she took the train to Salt Lake City and convinced the bankers to give her a loan. Emma was confident that she would sell a lot of wool because the WWI soldiers needed it for their uniforms.

Over time, Emma Yearian owned the largest western ranch among women landowners. She went on to be a state legislator and was named the "Sheep Queen of Idaho."

Zinc is used for galvanizing. Iron and steel are covered with a thin layer of zinc to prevent rust. Rocks containing zinc are often found with silver and lead. At one time, Idaho had the world's richest silver vein. The top producing mines were the Bunker Hill, Sunshine, and Hercules. Minerals are still important in Idaho. Mines throughout the state generate one billion dollars a year and keep many communities thriving. Although mining companies must use safe practices to keep soil and water clean, Idaho provides a wealth of resources.

Legend has it that the Bunker Hill mine was discovered by a donkey. Noah Kellogg was prospecting on a hill in north Idaho when his donkey kicked loose a shiny gray rock. The old prospector recognized it as galena ore, rich with silver and lead. Kellogg and his partners claimed ownership of the Bunker Hill mine, but they gave credit for its discovery to the donkey.

Z is for Zinc, a useful rock.
Idaho mines produce a lot.
If you want to keep the rust away,
a coating of zinc is the very best way.

Zz

A Vast Landscape Full of Facts

1. What river is the longest undammed river in the lower 48 states and is often called the River of No Return?

2. The largest forest of _____ _____ _____ in the United States can be found in Northern Idaho.

3. _____ was a most valuable friend to the Corps of Discovery.

4. The official nickname for Idaho is Potato State. True or false?

5. What town in Idaho was the first in the world to be powered by atomic energy?

6. She is the only female who designed a state seal.

7. Which two Idaho Native American tribes provided supplies to the Corps of Discovery for the challenging trip across the Rocky Mountains?

8. What is Idaho's state bird?

9. The discovery of _____ changed Idaho forever.

10. Hells Canyon is the deepest canyon in the United States. True or false?

11. The world's first chairlift was built in what Idaho resort?

12. They were the first people in the United States to develop selective breeding of horses.

13. A Quinceanera is a traditional celebration that began with the Aztec peoples. True or false?

14. The farmland around this city grows more potatoes than any other place in the United States.

15. The father of television grew up in Rigby, Idaho. What is his name?

16. What caused Mount Borah, Idaho's tallest peak, to grow one foot in 1983?

17. The World Center for _____ ___ _____ is located in Idaho.

18. Txistu (che-stu) is a three-holed recorder brought to America by what group of people?

19. Who was known as the "Sheep Queen of Idaho?"

20. Star garnets, the Idaho state gem, are found in only two places in the world: Idaho and _____.

Answers

1. Salmon River
2. Western white pine
3. Sacajawea
4. False. Idaho's nickname is the Gem State.
5. Arco
6. Emma Edwards Green
7. Lemhi Shoshone and Nez Perce
8. Mountain bluebird
9. Gold
10. True. Hells Canyon is deeper than the Grand Canyon of Arizona.

11. Sun Valley
12. Nez Perce
13. True. This coming-of-age Latina celebration for girls occurs at age 15.
14. Blackfoot
15. Philo T. Farnsworth
16. An earthquake that reached 7.3 on the Richter scale.
17. Birds of Prey
18. Basque
19. Emma Yearian
20. India

Stan and Joy Steiner

Author and university professor Stan Steiner has been nicknamed "The Bookman" by his Boise State University students because of his vast knowledge of children's literature and his ability to inspire them with reading. Joy makes storytelling magic wherever she goes. She performs, listens, and uses storytelling to make writing easier for students of all ages. Joy and Stan had great fun exploring and camping with their children throughout beautiful Idaho as they gathered information for *P is for Potato*. Visit Joy at www.joysteiner.com and visit Stan at http://education.boisestate.edu/stansteiner.

Jocelyn Slack

Jocelyn's childhood memories include a home filled with canvases, sculptures, and the smell of turpentine and oil paints. She was allowed to work on many projects with her mom's wonderful array of artist's materials. Jocelyn attended the California College of Arts and Crafts in Oakland, California and studied for several summers at the Banff School of Fine Arts in Alberta, Canada.

Jocelyn divides her time between Garden Valley, Idaho on the South Fork of the Payette River and Wilson, Wyoming. Her work as an artist has included murals, sandblasted glass, magazine illustration, logo design, and T-shirt and fabric design. She also produces limited edition prints.

She and her husband love to ski, run rivers, and hike. They have a daughter, Luna, two cats, and nine chickens.